Sisterhood

for the women who shaped me,

my soul sisters

Sisterhood

ILLUSTRATED BY
SARAH CRAY

GIBBS SMITH
TO ENRICH AND INSPIRE HUMANKIND

A LOYAL SISTER IS WORTH A THOUSAND FRIENDS.

FEMALE FRIENDSHIPS ARE JUST A HOP TO

OUR SISTERHOOD, AND SISTERHOOD CAN BE

A VERY POWERFUL FORCE . . .

Tanja Taaljard

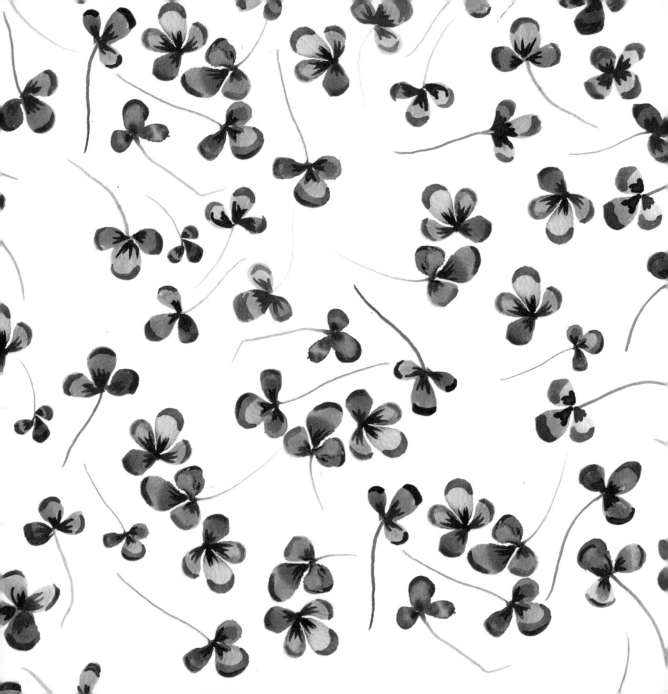

A good friend is like a four-leaf clover: hard to find and lucky to have.

IRISH PROVERB

A FRIEND IS ONE THAT KNOWS YOU AS YOU ARE, UNDERSTANDS WHERE YOU HAVE BEEN, ACCEPTS WHAT YOU HAVE BECOME, AND STILL, GENTLY ALLOWS YOU TO GROW.

For there is no friend like a sister in calm or stormy weather.

CHRISTINA ROSSETTI

A sister is both your mirror—

and your opposite.

ELIZABETH FISHEL

NO ONE UNDERSTANDS US LIKE US

ALEX ELLE

You can kid the world,

but not your sister.

CHARLOTTE GRAY

Friendship marks a life

even more deeply than love.

ELIE WIESEL

FRIENDSHIP IS BORN AT THAT MOMENT WHEN
ONE PERSON SAYS TO ANOTHER,

"What! You, too? I thought I was the only one."

C. S. LEWIS

Friendship is always a sweet responsibility, never an opportunity.

KHALIL GIBRAN

IN MY FRIEND,

I FIND A SECOND SELF.

Isabelle Norton

And like a favorite old movie,
sometimes the sameness
in a friend is what you like
the most about her.

EMILY GIFFIN,

SOMETHING BORROWED

FRIENDSHIP
HAPPINESS, AND
BY DOUBLING
DIVIDING

Marcus Tullius Cicero

IMPROVES
ABATES MISERY,
OUR JOYS AND
OUR GRIEF.

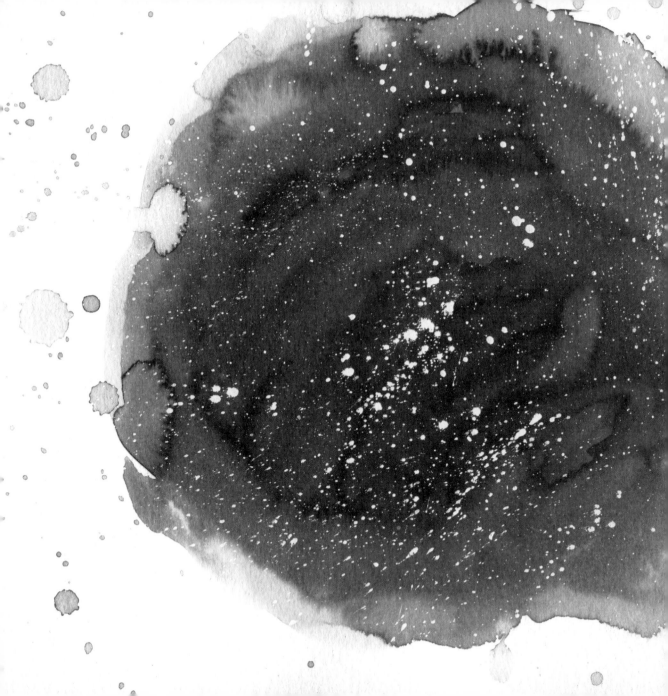

There is nothing like puking with somebody to make you into old friends.

SYLVIA PLATH,
THE BELL JAR

A sister is a forever friend.
A forever friend is a sister.

There is nothing I would not do for those who are really my friends. I have no notion of loving people by halves, it is not my nature.

JANE AUSTEN,

NORTHANGER ABBEY

Some people go to
priests, others to poetry,
I to my friends.

VIRGINA WOOLF

Friendship is the
not career or housework,
and it needs to be

...most important thing—

...r one's fatigue—

...tended and nurtured.

JULIA CHILD,
MY LIFE IN FRANCE

NOT ALL SISTERS ARE
BORN TO US, LIFE SAVES SOME
FOR ALONG THE WAY.

*Happiness is a cup of tea
and a chat with
my sister.*

The language of friendship is not words but meanings.

HENRY DAVID THOREAU

Be slow to fall into friendship;
but when thou art in, continue firm
and constant.

SOCRATES

Sisters are like thighs.
They stick together.

True friends are like diamonds—bright, beautiful, valuable and always in style.

NICOLE RICHIE

Sister time is good for the soul.

I'm so thankful for friendship. It beautifies life so much.

L. M. MONTGOMERY,
ANNE OF AVONLEA

One's life has value so long as one attributes value to the life of others, by means of love, friendship, and compassion.

SIMONE DE BEAUVOIR

It's the friends
you can call up at
4 a.m. that
matter.

MARLENE DIETRICH

SISTERS ARE DIFFERENT

FLOWERS FROM

THE SAME GARDEN

When I say I won't
tell anyone,
my sister doesn't count.

A sister is a gift to the heart, a friend to the spirit, a golden thread to the meaning of life.

ISADORA JAMES

SIDE BY SIDE, OR MILES APART,

SISTERS WILL ALWAYS BE CONNECTED BY THE HEART.

The most beautiful discovery true friends make is that they can grow separately without growing apart.

ELIZABETH FOLEY

One friend with whom you have a lot in common is better than three with whom you struggle to find things to talk about.

MINDY KALING,

IS EVERYONE HANGING OUT WITHOUT ME?

The best thing to hold onto in life
is each other.

AUDREY HEPBURN

A woman without her sister is like a bird without wings.

Friendship is the only cement that will ever hold the world together.

WOODROW T. WILSON

SISTERS DON'T NEED
WORDS, THEY HAVE
PERFECTED THEIR OWN
SECRET LANGUAGE OF
SMILES, SNIFFS, SIGHS,
GASPS, WINKS
AND EYE ROLLS.

Friendship however is a plant which cannot be forced — true friendship is no gourd spring up in a night and withering in a day.

CHARLOTTE BRONTË,

THE LETTERS OF CHARLOTTE BRONTË

Is solace anywhere more comforting than that in the arms of a sister?

ALICE WALKER

friendship IS a slow RIPENING fruit

ARISTOTLE

Sisters in battle,
I am shield and blade to you.

LEIGH BARDUGO,
WONDER WOMAN: WARBRINGER

We are friends for life. When we're together the years fall away. Isn't that what matters? To have someone who can remember with you? To have someone who remembers how far you've come?

JUDY BLUME

Sister. . . . She is your partner in crime, your midnight companion, someone who knows when you are smiling, even in the dark.

BARBARA ALPERT

The friend who holds your hand and says the wrong thing is made of dearer stuff than the one who stays away.

BARBARA KINGSOLVER

There's one thing
stronger than magic

Sisterhood

ROBIN BENWAY,

THE EXTRAORDINARY SECRETS OF APRIL, MAY, AND JUNE

My friends have made the story of my life. In a thousand ways they have turned my limitations into beautiful privileges.

HELEN KELLER

The best mirror is an old friend.

GEORGE HERBERT

Women understand.
We may share experiences, make jokes, paint pictures, and describe humiliations that mean nothing to men, but women understand.

GLORIA STEINEM

WOMEN ARE GOING TO
FORM A CHAIN, A
GREATER SISTERHOOD
THAN THE WORLD HAS
EVER KNOWN.

Nellie McClung

Friends change, lovers leave, sisters are eternal.

SARAH CRAY IS A WATERCOLOR ARTIST, WIFE, AND MOTHER OF TWO DAUGHTERS. SHE GRADUATED MAGNA CUM LAUDE FROM SACRAMENTO STATE IN 2015 WITH A DEGREE IN ART STUDIO, EMPHASIS IN PAINTING AND DRAWING, AND NOW RESIDES IN MISSOURI. SHE HAS BEEN CREATING CUSTOM WATERCOLOR AND ACRYLIC PAINTINGS SINCE 2013, GROWING A SMALL SIDE BUSINESS INTO HER DREAM CAREER. ALONG WITH BEING A FREELANCE ILLUSTRATOR, CRAY HAS CREATED "LET'S MAKE ART," AN ONLINE COMMUNITY AND ART SUPPLY SHOP, WITH THE GOAL OF GETTING MORE PEOPLE TO PAINT AND LIVE A MORE CREATIVE LIFE. SISTERHOOD IS HER SECOND BOOK.